The
FORTUNE
COOKIE
Book

A Little Food For Thought

RUNNING PRESS
PHILADELPHIA · LONDON

A Running Press® Miniature Edition™
© 2001 by Running Press

Library of Congress Cataloging-in-Publication Number 2001086966

ISBN 0-7624-1086-8

This book may be ordered by mail from the publisher.
Please include $1.00 for postage and handling.
But try your bookstore first!

Running Press Book Publishers
125 South Twenty-second Street
Philadelphia, Pennsylvania 19103-4399

Visit us on the web!
www.runningpress.com

You will
reach the highest
possible point
in your business
or profession.

You

can

always

find

a way

out.

Avoid pressing
a situation.

Personal insight
requires acknowledging one's
shortcomings.

Have the courage
to take your own thoughts
seriously.

It is very difficult to prophesize, especially when it pertains to the future.

Change
your
thoughts
and you
will
change
your
world.

The
answer
to
your
question
is
yes.

You have
the power to
influence
all with whom
you come
in contact.

You plan things
that you don't even
attempt because
of your extreme
consciousness of what
others may think.

Everything before you is only your perception.

Flow with the day's events.

Your mind
will go through a
period of considerable
expansion.

You are
an untapped
source of
talent
and creativity.

Take responsibility
for your greatness.

Sin has many tools,
but a lie is the handle
that fits them all.

The nail that sticks up gets
hammered down.

What are
you waiting for?

The light at the end of the tunnel could mean bad things.

You are adored by many
and loathed by none.

Never stop
at the weigh
station
on the road
to life.

There is great temptation in store for you.

The path of least resistance is always the most arduous.

Your greatest enemy is keeping
a close watch on you.

Talk candidly with
your mate; the truth will
be encouraging.

Relaxing music
helps to make the right
decision.

Versatility is one of your
outstanding traits.

You take an optimistic view of life.

Spice up your
appearance and love
will be waiting.

Watch

what

you

say.

There's a good chance of a romantic encounter soon.

Rest is a good thing, but
boredom is its brother.

Speak
out
about
issues
that
concern
you.

A good evening is one
spent in good company.

You will be given a post of trust and responsibility.

Keep a level head
in a crisis.

Control your temper
and the world is yours.

New professional opportunities
are moneymakers.

Do not take
your love for granted.
Especially now.

Don't be hasty;
prosperity will knock on
your door soon.

Aspire to achieve;
you're almost there.

This is your lucky week to attend to a legal matter.

Failure is
the mother
of success.

You are
contemplating
some action which
will bring credit
upon you.

You will
be recognized
and honored
as a community
leader.

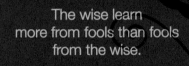

The wise learn
more from fools than fools
from the wise.

Actions speak louder than words; express yourself.

You have a deep appreciation
for the arts and music.

Work
to
balance
your
love
of
money.

Sell
unwanted
goods.

You are a perfectionist;
don't spoil it.

Ask for what you need
with a whisper. It works!

You will meet a person
who can change your life.

Go shopping
with a bargain-hunter.

The only rose
without a thorn is friendship.

Aim for a
compromise.

Work smarter, not harder.

Even on a cloudy day,
the sun still rises.

You

can

always

find

a

way

out.

Manage your affairs with grace.
It will bring surprising results.

Fortunes often have multiple meanings—read them deeply.

You were right the first time.

You will reach
the highest possible
point in your business
or profession.

Happiness is a direction,
not a destination.

There are no paths;
paths are made by walking.

Be notorious today.

Accept compliments
and give praise.

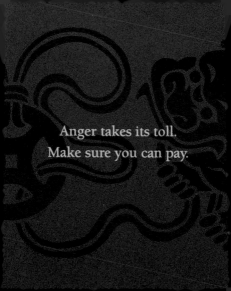

Anger takes its toll.
Make sure you can pay.

If you find yourself in a hole,
stop digging.

Love at first sight happens
most often in hindsight.

Don't turn back or you'll miss
your next turn.

Anger is revenge taken on yourself for another's misdeeds.

The
one
who
listens
is the
one
who
understands.

Others may doubt
what you say,
but they'll remember
what you do.

Your destiny isn't in chance
but in choice.

If the shoe fits, buy two pair.

The universe is energy that responds to expectations.

Be the change you wish
to see in your world.

The wise
count their blessings;
the foolish,
their problems.

When
you drink from
the stream,
remember the
source.

You have
a grand purpose.

Laugh at yourself and you can always be amused.

Sometimes even a fool
makes a good suggestion.

Don't blind others
with your blindness.

If you
cannot
change
your mind,
you cannot
change
anything.

Notice the small things and the world always seems large.

The best is yet to come.

You learn best by teaching.

Ask for more time before
making an important decision.

Avoid pity but strive
for compassion.

Procrastination
never ends.

Say what you mean and
mean what you say.

Give people more than they expect and do it cheerfully.

Don't judge people
by their relatives.

If you must pick the rose,
expect to get pricked.

When you lose,
don't lose the lesson.

Spend some time alone.

Open your arms
to change, but don't let
go of your values.

Work takes an
auspicious turn today.

Don't interrupt
when you are being flattered.

Read between the lines.

Be gentle
with the earth.

Mind your
own business.

One
asking
advice
is looking
for an
accomplice.

The best
relationship is
one in which
your love for each
other is greater than
your need
for each other.

Your character
is your destiny.

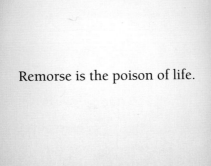

Remorse is the poison of life.

None of us is as smart as all of us.

Be good;
if you're not good,
be careful.

Redemption is within
your grasp.

Wish

upon a

star

tonight.

Your tenacity shall
be rewarded.

Attention
naturally gravitates
toward you.

One who can forgive
will be rewarded with
inner peace.

Simplify.

Success is the best revenge.

The shape of a cloud
will bear a message to you.

Listen
carefully,
even when
no one
is talking.

This book has
been bound using handcraft
methods and Smyth-sewn
to ensure durability.

The dust jacket and interior were
designed by Frances J. Soo Ping Chow.

The text was edited by Molly Jay.

Photographs by Michael Weiss.

The text was set in
ITC Berkeley, Helvetica Light,
and Koch-Antiqua.